This i

Effectively Praying for Your Husband When the Enemy Attacks

30 Life-Changing Prayers That Transformed My Husband and My Marriage

Dee Johnson, LCSW

MW00935159

No part of this publication may be reproduced, stored in a retrieval system or transmitted in any way by any means, electronic, mechanical, photocopy, recording or otherwise without the prior permission of the author except as provided by USA copyright law.

This book is designed to provide accurate and authoritative information with regard to the subject matter covered. This information is given with the understanding that the author is not engaged in rendering legal or professional advice. Since the details of your situation are fact dependent, you should additionally seek the services of a competent professional.

Copyright © 2018 Dee Johnson.

All rights reserved.

www.WifeNation.Com

www.IAmDeeJohnson.com

ISBN-13: 978-1983854620
ISBN-10: 198385462X

Dedication

I would like to dedicate this to my wonderful, supportive husband,

Mr. Earnest E. Johnson, Jr.

Thank you for allowing me to be your wife and life partner.

Contents

Preface

The purpose of this book is to help wives develop a strategy for effectively fighting the enemy when the enemy is attempting to destroy her husband and marriage. This book is a personal collection of the very prayers that I prayed over my husband and my marriage when it seemed as if my family was being destroyed and divorce was imminent. I almost lost my battle. I almost walked away. But God told me to stay in the fight and develop a new strategy, and He would turn everything around in our favor. I won't lie, it was the toughest fight of my life. I have never prayed so much. I have never experienced so much pain. I often felt like I would crumble under the pressure of the weight. I wasn't convinced that any of it was worth the amount of sacrifice, frustration, disappointment, or pain I was experiencing. But since God made me a promise, I had to find the courage to dig deeper and to go through this process. For me, change began taking shape over the course of about 30 days. For you, it may take less time or it may take longer. There is no deadline for this journey. You can pray these prayers every 30 days until you see the changes that you are believing God to make in your husband and marriage. These prayers and life lessons are timeless. They were birthed from raw emotion and came from the deepest crevices of my being. I was literally crying out to God and I believe they have the transformative power to help you get your happily ever after. Thank you for trusting me to help you walk this journey with you.

Introduction

"Be clear-minded and alert. Your opponent, the devil, is prowling around like a roaring lion, looking for someone to devour" (1 Peter 5:8).

This scripture will be mentioned several times throughout this book because it provides such powerful illustration on the type of opponent you are facing as you fight to save your husband and marriage.

Please take a moment to imagine a lion on the prowl. Imagine that lion hunting, roaring, targeting a specific prey, sizing up his prey, and figuring out a strategy to overtake and conquer his intended target. This is what is happening right now. The enemy has set his sights on your husband and he has every intention of fighting to the finish.

This is the type of enemy you are up against.

A roaring lion causes fear.

A roaring lion causes people to run, hide and take cover.

A roaring lion causes people to lose focus on what is in front of them because they are so fearful of the damage the lion is threatening to do to them.

That's exactly how the enemy wants you to feel and react to what is going on around you. He wants you to be so fearful and intimidated that you can't fight back. His strategy is to attack the leader so that there is no defense for the home, family, or marriage. He will often use women, addictions, past hurts, feelings of inadequacies, or other people as bait to help keep your spouse entangled.

Once there is chaos, disruption, pain, and bitterness, he works on the wife's emotions and continues to use whatever or whoever is influencing the leader to keep the life partners separated—emotionally or physically. He knows that two are stronger than one (Ecclesiastes 4:9). He knows his plan will work more effectively if there is division. So he lays traps and plants seeds. That's why the Bible tells us to be on guard, be sober minded (1 Peter 5:8), and take thoughts captive (2 Corinthians 10:5) so we don't fall into his hidden traps. Once the leader and co-leader of the home are distracted, he can find an opening into the kids' lives while the leaders are focusing on their own pain and licking their own wounds. That's one way generational curses form. Generational curse is another word for bondage—spiritual, mental, emotional, physical, and financial bondage. And the mentality gets passed on to the kids who pass it on to their kids who pass it on to their kids.

The solution is warfare.

A Word about War

This is War!

We don't play small.

We don't cower in the corner and hide.

 We don't keep crying ourselves to sleep.

We show up, armed spiritually and ready to defend and protect what is ours.

We pray, worship, get counseling, meditate on the word of God, read marriage books (and books about conflict resolution and communication), get support from like-minded individuals, deal with our own stuff, apologize, forgive, surrender, study, and show respect.

Please understand, dear wife that the enemy is a formidable opponent and not to be underestimated.

Things may get worse before they get better as the enemy turns up the heat.

You will be discouraged.

You will be tempted to give up.

You will be challenged in ways you never thought possible.

War means an "armed conflict" between two sides.

You are fighting *for* your husband and marriage while the enemy is fighting *against* your husband and marriage.

Make sure you respect the enemy's level of determination in keeping things the way he wants them and expect the fight of your life! Sometimes you will feel as if you are the only one fighting and your husband is working against you. It will seem unfair. It will seem as if God has forgotten to send someone to help fight for you. I have been there. But consider this.

When a soldier is wounded while in combat, his comrades don't leave him there to die or to be taken captive by the other forces. They drag him to safety. Right now, you are that comrade that God is asking to help drag your husband to safety.

Picture your husband as a POW (Prisoner of War). He is in captivity and he doesn't know how to get set free. He is in bondage. He's in the grips of the enemy. He doesn't have what it takes to get free on his own. He needs your help.

God knows you are hurting. God knows that you're in pain and it feels as if the bottom has fallen out. God told me when I was feeling this way, the bottom has to fall out in order to get my attention to the fact that battle is raging around me, and it isn't time to slumber. Sometimes the bottom falls out to show you what you're up against spiritually. Isn't it better to know your enemy so you can develop a strategy? The bottom falls out so it can expose your real battle. As long as things are going well, deliverance, healing and restoration are not necessary. But once the enemy is exposed, you can formulate a game plan. It's not always because it's time to walk away from your marriage. It's to show you that you aren't wrestling against flesh and blood. Sometimes it's not to destroy you but to get you to a new level in life and to help you get your prayers answered regarding your husband and marriage. As long as things are going well, you'd never seek God on the level you need to. That's why he allows the bottom to fall out!

Gearing up for Battle

1. Get rid of all distractions including social media and other people. You need to stay laser-focused.

2. Shift your focus inward. Understand that the only person you can control is yourself. Stop focusing on what your hubby is/is not doing and turn your focus on how you may please God and what He wants you to do. It will be necessary to surrender your plans, your ways, your habits, and your thoughts towards pleasing God.

3. Realize that you are the solution to your own happiness. You don't have to wait until your relationship issues are resolved in order to be happy, whole, and complete. If you think you do, that means you've given another human being power over your life and the power to dictate your own personal sense of fulfillment.

4. Acknowledge the pain so you can get past it. Denial invalidates the pain and delays healing. Yes, relationship issues are a struggle. Yes, relationship issues are uncomfortable and can wreck havoc on you emotionally, mentally, spiritually, etc. Yet you can get past all of the pain that you've suffered up until this point.

5. Make a plan to deal with the pain. Dealing with it gives God room to give you clarity. Pain clutters the mind. It takes over the emotions. Pain causes cloudiness so you can't expect to get clear

on what your next steps should be as long as you are babysitting your pain.

And your pain is valid. I'm not minimizing that at all; but you get to choose how long you stay in pain and what impact the pain has on you.

6. Don't let your pain change who you are at the core. If you've always been a sweet person, continue to be sweet. If you've always been kind and generous, continue to be kind and generous. Let it burn away all of the things that need to change. Let it mature you in ways you need to mature. Let it have its perfect work so you will come out better on the other side. Understand that nothing grows or transforms without pain, discomfort, and challenges. Don't become bitter, angry, or hostile. Stay true to yourself.

7. Let God change you. Realize that it's more about you than you think. Your focus is on your spouse; God's focus is on you and your hubby. God's not going to grow, change, and mature your husband without you growing, changing, and maturing also. You have to learn how to deal with the new him. You have to break certain patterns in your behavior and thoughts to fit who he is becoming and not hold him hostage to who he has always been. Don't see him as a liability, rather see him as your opportunity to grow into the woman God designed you to be.

8. Get control over your thought life. If left unchecked, your mind will get you into trouble, keep you in bondage, and wreak havoc on your emotions. You must control your thought life at all times. Your thought can also be the catalyst for your breakthrough. I had to realize that I pray for a lot of things daily and God answers just about all of them daily like health, protection, etc. We have a tendency to focus on the prayers that God isn't answering instead of thanking Him for all of the prayers He is answering.

9. Recognize the blessing in this situation. Your pain is actually a gift that has opened your heart to God on a level that it never has. It has shown you how to ask for help instead of thinking you have to do everything on your own. It has humbled you...we know we have to be humble before God will exalt us. It has strengthened your prayer life. It has made you focus on what's really important and worthy of your time, energy, and attention. It has birthed a ministry. It has birthed books. It has birthed friendships you would have never had. It has strengthened you. It has matured you. My husband's actions and the subsequent pain pushed me to fall on my face before God. The experience forced me to change, pushed me into my destiny, and set me on the path leading to my purpose. The pain is a gift. Think of the story of Joseph and all he went through with his family betraying him and all of the injustices he experienced before God blessed him beyond his expectations. Think of the Israelites and how they

went from slavery, to escape slavery and get to the Promised Land. You want the promise without the pain and that is not what we are taught in Scripture. There is always pain before the promise. ALWAYS. Think of Jesus and all He went through to get to God's promise. David was told he would be king while he was a child but had to tend to sheep, fight Goliath, and get threats of death from Saul before he could take his position on the throne. Look at Sarah, Hannah, and Rachel. They had to wait years before God opened their wombs. There was pain of watching other women give birth and mother children before they received their promise. So you won't ever get your promise without going through pain. Let Scripture encourage you that the pain was worth waiting on the promise.

10. Treat him like a king even when he's acting like a peasant. We reap what we sow so ensure what you sow is what you want to reap. God is watching. It's God's promise that we will reap if we faint not! The goal is to bring out his best and you can't do that if you are treating him badly.

11. Have a safe place to vent and get support. It may be a support group or a close mature friend. This journey can seem overwhelming and can get lonely at times. You need a safe outlet.

12. Give 100% even when you feel slighted. Talk to God about the unfairness of it all. Vent to your support system about it all. But

you can't have 1 foot in and 1 foot out the door and expect to be victorious. Treat him the way you want him to treat you. Show him how to love by how you love him. Love is patient, kind, humble, etc.

13. Everything you want in life takes sacrifice and hard work. Some days will be filled with tears and frustration. Some days you will feel weak and question whether or not it's worth it. Losing weight, building a business, being a parent, and transforming your marriage all require sacrifice, consistency, and hard work.

14. Stop keeping track of his mistakes. It serves no purpose once you've decided to fight for your marriage. You can't pull this off from a place of bitterness, anger, and resentment. That doesn't mean you aren't entitled to have those feelings, you just won't be successful by operating from that negative mindset.

15. You are on a battlefield. If you turn your back and walk away before the enemy is defeated, you lose. You have no choice but to face the enemy head on. You can't hide. You can keep crying about it. In fact, too many emotions will get you killed during war time. Solider up!

16. Keep reminding yourself throughout this journey that pain and disappointment will not last forever. Every war must come to an end. I realized that my delays, disappointments, and

dissatisfaction caused me to begin to doubt God's promises to me. I was growing so weary and felt so weighed down that I began to question whether or not God really cared for me. I found myself sinking deeper into despair because things weren't happening when I envisioned or how I envisioned and because it was becoming too difficult to keep holding on to my faith. So my faith began to waver. My resolve began to get weak. I was contemplating if serving God's people and trying to follow God's plan was worth the physical, spiritual, emotional, and financial exhaustion that I couldn't seem to get from under. I struggled. I was at war. My flesh and my spirit were at odds and my flesh seemed to be at an advantage. I was fighting for my family. I was fighting for my ministry. I was fighting for my health. I was fighting for my sanity. I was at war, day in and day out. I tried listening to encouraging music and sermons but little was this making any significant difference. Then I remembered what God told me six months prior. He had warned me that war time was coming and He gave me a battle strategy. So I had to make a decision to follow His strategy when in my eyes, it seemed insufficient for what I was going through. He wanted me to worship and do faith confessions when I needed a financial break through and a renewed commitment in my marriage. I was seeking healing. I was seeking changes to my ministry. I was seeking changes on my job. I was seeking solutions for problems that God's strategy didn't seem to address. And because what He instructed didn't seem to fit the challenges I was facing, I became anxiety-ridden trying to figure out another solution. I began to question my relationship with God. I began to contemplate leaving the faith that has proven itself invaluable throughout the years. My unwillingness to follow God's strategy almost became my undoing. So I decided that I had nothing to lose and everything to gain. Besides, He wasn't telling me to do anything impossible. He just wanted me to worship even when my flesh didn't want to. He wanted me to call on the name of Jesus when I didn't have strength to fight, and to confess His word and promises over my family and speak His word to them in love. Not too much to ask. So I began to be consistent in worship. I heard Joel Osteen say "find God's promises in His word and began to recite them back to God," so I did that too. I was believing for great miracles and anxiously awaited for the manifestation of them. Remember, trouble doesn't last always.

MY PERSONAL CONFESSION

Right now I'm feeling:

_____

_____

_____

My biggest fear about this process is:

_____

_____

_____

What I hope to learn:

_____

_____

_____

My expectations about this process are:

_____

_____

_____

Commitment Statement

Lord, I am fully committing myself to this process. I know that you want me to fight for this relationship like never before so I can see results that I've never seen before. I will be intentional with my words, attitudes, and body language and will not allow myself to display anything that contradicts what I am trying to accomplish.

When I am in pain, I will keep my commitment.

When I'm confused, I will keep my commitment.

When I want to walk away, I will keep my commitment.

When my spouse offers resistance and works against this process and my commitment to change, I will keep my commitment.

I need your help, courage, guidance, gentleness, compassion, and strength during this time. I need you to raise God-fearing people to be a support to me during this time. I need help to stay committed. I'm so tired of trying to do this all on my own. I submit my will to your will and my plans to your plans. I am committed to doing this your way. If I get off track, quickly remind me of your expectations of me and help me to get back on track before I ruin any progress I may have made. This is my personal commitment to you.

A Wife's Battle Prayer

May your word be a lamp onto my feet and a light onto my path (Psalm 119:105). Show me how to effectively and consistently pray for my husband. Show me how to support him in a way that will be meaningful and impactful to him. Preserve my heart in righteousness that my words and actions please you at all times. Keep me safely tucked under your covering so the enemy can't get to me and hinder the work that you are calling me to complete. Strengthen me so I don't walk away from my assignment prematurely and miss what you have in store for me. Show me how to be your soldier during this battle.

Day 1

His Identity in Christ

Lord, my husband is struggling with his identity in Christ. Assure him that he is adequate. Assure him that he is worthy of your love and forgiveness. Help him to overcome his pain, obstacles, doubt, fears, and worries and show him how to forgive himself so that he can be set free from the bondage that has crippled him throughout the years. Don't allow the enemy to steal anymore time and peace from him. Show him how to rest in your love for him. Show him how to look, lean, and depend on you to get all of his needs met. May he not fall victim to the opinions of others but may his desire be to please you and you alone. Strengthen him at all times. Grant him your peace, presence, provision, and protection at all times. May you always be enough to meet all of his needs and fill in any gaps in his life so he doesn't look for validation from human hands. Come along beside him and heal him, nurture him, strengthen him, deliver him, help him, and guide him. Meet needs that he didn't know he had, fill in gaps he didn't realize existed, and bind wounds that refuse to heal. Be his everything at all times, in every situation. Show him a clear vision of what you have called him to be and help him to walk in that calling. Show him how great of man he is and give him the confidence to walk in that greatness. Show him an accurate picture of you so he has an accurate picture of himself. Correct any errors with his self-identity and may he become a new creature in Christ (2 Corinthians 5:17). In Jesus' name, I pray. Amen.

Wisdom for Wives

Breathe life into your husband by offering unconditional respect. You have the ability to resuscitate your relationship by respecting your husband. In fact, respect is probably the most important thing you can do and a crucial first step in getting your relationship on track.

Disrespect deflates. Disrespect emasculates. Disrespect renders a man spiritually, emotionally, mentally, and sometimes physically impotent. You will never have the type of husband you desire if you are disrespectful towards him.

War Weapon: Ephesians 5:33b (AMP)

"And let the wife see that she respects *and* reverences her husband (that she notices him, regards him, honors him, prefers him, venerates, and esteems him; and that she defers to him, praises him, and loves and admires him exceedingly)."

My thoughts/feelings about today:

_____

_____

_____

This is War

Day 2

His Decision Making

God, help my husband to stop making fear-based decisions. The fear of failure, fear of being seen as less than perfect, fear of what other people have to say, fear of what may happen, and fear of rejection are keeping him from becoming the husband that you envisioned. Instead, may he make rational, wisdom-based decisions, with a mindset based on integrity, fidelity, righteousness, and fear of the Lord. Sear the potential consequences of any decision that will negatively affect his family in his heart and mind, so it will keep him on the right path. Keep him when he doesn't want to be kept and deliver him from the hands and plans of the enemy. Teach him to fear your name so he can receive the benefits that come from the fear of the Lord.

According to your word,

The fear of the LORD adds length to life (Proverbs 10:27a)

Through the fear of the LORD evil is avoided (Proverbs 16:6b)

I want my husband to respect your wishes so he doesn't make decisions that will position him to lose his family, finances, peace, health, or future. But only you have the power to ensure that doesn't happen. So I'm seeking you on behalf of my husband. In Jesus' name, I pray. Amen.

Wisdom for Wives

Control your tongue and only speak life-giving words. The Bible tells us that life and death are in the power of the tongue (Proverbs 18:21). God's desire is that we speak life to any dead places that occupy space in our husband's life. So learn to control your tongue and allow your words to raise your husband from the dead.

War Weapon: Ephesians 4:29

"Let no corrupting talk come out of your mouths, but only such as is good for building up, as fits the occasion, that it may give grace to those who hear."

My thoughts/feelings about today

_____

_____

_____

_____

_____

_____

_____

_____

Day 3

His Pain

Lord, my husband has been hurt in unimaginable ways. My husband has been betrayed and disappointed. My husband has experienced pain that has influenced him and changed him in ways he cannot face or admit. I know you as Jehovah Rapha, my healer (Psalm 30:2). I'm asking you to heal my husband as well. Heal him from the burden that this pain has created. Bind every wound. Don't allow this pain to color his view of you, others, or himself any longer. May he cry out to you when his soul gets weary. Please hear the cries of his heart and offer deliverance, peace, comfort, and a safe haven to him even when he doesn't say anything about the condition of his soul. Speak to the wounds that keep him in turmoil and keep him confused and questioning who he is. Speak to every broken and shattered place in his life and give him a new, mature perspective on how to find purpose from his pain. I speak against the wounds from his past that is affecting his present and has the potential to negatively affect his future. I speak wholeness, completeness, forgiveness, feelings of worthiness, and high self-regard over my husband. I stand in agreement with your word which says no weapon formed against him will prosper (Isaiah 54:17). Help him to stand strong despite the pain. Give him the courage to face the pain. Give him the support to work through the pain. And most importantly, heal him completely of the pain. In Jesus' Name, I pray. Amen.

Wisdom for Wives

Don't keep punishing him. Don't do it your own way. He won't get healed that way. He needs acceptance, not just tolerance. He can't handle rejection. Understand how his past experiences have shaped him and kept him in bondage. Don't make this worse for him. See him as a patient with cancer if you must. He got the disease through no fault of his own and he doesn't know how to heal.

War Weapon: Titus 3:2

"To speak evil of no one, to avoid quarreling, to be gentle, and to show perfect courtesy toward all people."

My thoughts/feelings about today

_____

_____

_____

_____

_____

_____

_____

Day 4

His Strength to Resist Temptation

God, I'm praying for you to help my husband to resist temptation. May he be wise enough to put safeguards in place to help him deal with and avoid temptation. May he recognize that the enemy will use his temptations to destroy his life and may he be strong enough and wise enough to run when he is tempted. When he is tempted to engage in activities that would displease you, quickly show him a picture of the consequences if he gives in to his temptation. May he understand that he should flee, not flirt with temptation and that he will never be strong enough to withstand it on a long-term basis. Don't let him fall prey to anymore traps. Give him wisdom and discernment that will keep him during those times when he doesn't want to be kept. Run after him and overtake him with your mercy, grace, and favor. Grow him up in you so he can become all that you envisioned. Keep the hands of the enemy off him. Give him your perspective and be his conscience at all times. Make him uncomfortable when he sins. Make him restless when he doesn't repent. In Jesus name, I pray. Amen.

Wisdom for Wives

It's easy to love someone when he is easy to love, but the vow says "for better or worse." So, commitment to the vow means sticking it out when things aren't easy (except abusive situations—God doesn't want you to be a punching bag or risk your life), when your husband is not easy to love, and when it would be easier to just walk away. That's commitment! That's marriage! And that's what you signed up for! So, honor your vow. Pay what you owe. Here is your hope:

"Those who sow with tears will reap with songs of joy. Those who go out weeping, carrying seed to sow, will return with songs of joy, carrying sheaves with them" Psalm 126:5-6 (NIV).

War Weapon: Deuteronomy 23:21, 23

"If you make a vow to the LORD your God, do not be slow to pay it, for the LORD your God will certainly demand it of you and you will be guilty of sin. Whatever your lips utter you must be sure to do, because you made your vow freely to the LORD your God with your own mouth."

My thoughts/feelings about today

_____

_____

_____

_____

_____

_____

_____

Day 5

His Value

I pray for his self-esteem and the sense of value that he has for himself. I pray that he would come to recognize and understand how valuable you deem him to be. I pray that the schemes, plots, and plans of the enemy would be destroyed and no longer have influence over his life. I pray that he sees his value and walks in his calling and not be led astray at any time. I pray that you would raise him up emotionally, spiritually, financially, mentally, and physically and be the source of strength, power, and encouragement that he needs. Shower him with your unconditional love and may he perceive it every day of his life. Don't allow the lies of the enemy to penetrate his self-esteem, change his view of you, or destroy what you want to accomplish in his life. May he begin to view his growing pains as a necessary part of life to position him to excel. May he not run when times get too tough. May you birth the level of maturity he needs to become the man you created. In Jesus name, I pray. Amen.

Wisdom for Wives

The word *exodus* means to exit or leave. You cannot stay in the same mindset and interacting the same way and expect to get the answer to your prayers. It is imperative that you exit from where you are to where you want to be. There will be times of "manna" when you'll feel like you are barely surviving (Exodus 16:4). There will be times when the enemy is hot on your trail trying to destroy you (Exodus 14:9). There will be times when you are tempted to go back to where you came from because at least you know what to expect back there (Numbers 14:3). There will be giants when you're almost to the Promised Land. (Numbers 13:31) There will be people who won't make it to the Promised Land with you. This is all a part of the journey towards a new, improved marriage. Don't expect this journey to be easy. Don't expect the enemy to give up without a fight! Remember, this is War!

War Weapon: 1 Corinthians 9:24

"Do you not know that in a race all the runners run, but only one gets the prize? Run in such a way as to get the prize."

My thoughts/feelings about today

_____

_____

_____

_____

_____

_____

_____

Day 6

His Perspective about Marriage

Lord, I pray that you would change my husband's mindset about marriage. May his thoughts and heart's convictions line up with your Word. Give him a clear picture of what you intended marriage to be and help him to become a great husband to me. I know your desire is for us to grow old together but there is some healing, forgiving, and changing that has to be done in order for that to happen. May he seek the counsel and support of godly men who have learned what it takes to have a great marriage. May he learn to honor me as his wife. May he recognize my value in his life and not take it for granted or be dismissive of it (Proverbs 18:22). May he see me the same way Adam saw Eve when he first laid eyes on her (Genesis 2:23). May he lust after me like David lusted after Bathsheba when he first laid eyes on her (2 Samuel 11:2). May he cover me and stand by me as Joseph did for Mary when he questioned how she became pregnant with Jesus (Matthew 1:18-25). May he work to have me with the same level of intensity as Jacob did to make Rachel his wife (Genesis 29:20, 29:27-28). May he be as committed to me and this marriage as Prophet Hosea was to Gomer (the Book of Hosea). In Jesus name, I pray. Amen.

Wisdom for Wives

There is too much at stake for you to walk away. There is too much to lose and too many people that will be affected if you walk away. Draw your strength from God. Engage in self-care activities. Pamper yourself. You are going through a lot right now. This is a difficult time for you. Ensure your needs are taken care of.

War Weapon: Mark 6:30-32

The apostles gathered around Jesus and reported to him all they had done and taught. Then, because so many people were coming and going that they did not even have a chance to eat, he said to them, "Come with me by yourselves to a quiet place and get some rest." So they went away by themselves in a boat to a solitary place.

My thoughts/feelings about today

_____

_____

_____

_____

_____

_____

_____

Day 7

His Vision for the Future

God, I'm praying that my husband's eyes be enlightened. Open his eyes so that he may see your truth. I pray that he sees you and that he sees the path that is pleasing to you. Give him a vision of his future and show him how to reach his destiny. May he see my love and commitment towards him. May he see the importance of him leading this family, serving you, and walking circumspectly at all times. Take the scales from his eyes. Reveal to him the benefits of living for you. Show him a new way of thinking and behaving; give him a taste of true freedom and may it be so pleasant to him that he chases after freedom in Christ for the rest of his life. Open his eyes to see how his decisions affect his children and me. Don't let him be blinded any longer. I pray that he sees himself as you created him. Let him see how great of a man you created him to be. Help him to accept that you don't make mistakes and took special care to create him. May he not allow his worldly experiences, the words of others, or his perceptions of his shortcomings color his view of himself. Show him the king that resides inside of him. Point him to your Word so he'll know that you created him a little lower than the angels (Hebrews 2:7). Reveal yourself to him so he will know that he was created in your image (Genesis 1:27) and begin to walk in a way that is worthy of his crown. In Jesus name, I pray. Amen.

Wisdom for Wives

Make a commitment to minister to your husband by being kind and respectful. Regardless of how he's acting or what he says, honor him as your spouse. Commit to bringing all of your concerns, doubts, fear, and complaints about him to the throne of God. Do not contribute to his downfall by partnering with the enemy to destroy him. Do not criticize him to his face or behind his back. Do not tell him things that will crush his spirit and cause division. Do not choose to put others ahead of your relationship with him. He is your priority.

War Weapon: 1 Peter 3:1-4 (AMP)

"In the same way, you wives, be submissive to your own husbands [subordinate, not as inferior, but out of respect for the responsibilities entrusted to husbands and their accountability to God, and so partnering with them] so that even if some do not obey the word [of God], they may be won over [to Christ] without discussion by the *godly* lives of their wives, when they see your modest and respectful behavior [together with your devotion and appreciation—love your husband, encourage him, and enjoy him as a blessing from God]. Your adornment must not be *merely* external—with interweaving *and* elaborate knotting of the hair, and wearing gold jewelry, or [being superficially preoccupied with] dressing in *expensive* clothes; but let it be [the inner beauty of] the hidden person of the heart, with the imperishable quality *and* unfading charm of a gentle and peaceful spirit, [one that is calm and self-controlled, not overanxious, but serene and spiritually mature] which is very precious in the sight of God."

My thoughts/feelings about today

_____

_____

_____

_____

_____

_____

_____

Day 8

Fighting the Enemy

I command that every yoke that is keeping my husband weighed down be broken. The enemy can't have his identity! The enemy can't have his joy! The enemy can't have his mind! The enemy can't have his life! I command that every plot and plan that has erected itself against my husband is cancelled.

God, I partner my faith with your power against any scheme or wickedness that is threatening to keep my husband in harm's way. Don't allow him to fall victim or prey to those that mean him harm. Open his eyes so that he may see and have discernment for every situation. Set the captive free from the chains of bondage and brokenness that has the potential to imprison his soul. Free him from the grips of despair, desperation, hopelessness, helplessness, and loneliness. May he enjoy the freedom and joy that comes from following your ways all the days of his life. Your word says, *"He whom the Lord sets free is free indeed"* (John 8:36; paraphrase). I'm relying on your Word. I have hope in your Word. My faith is strengthened by your Word. Do exactly what your Word promises to do. In the matchless name of Jesus, I pray. Amen.

Wisdom for Wives

If Satan had the nerve to wage war against God, what makes you think you're exempt? He will wage war against you too. And the war will get tougher the harder you fight! This journey will be uncomfortable and painful but it's very necessary. Your husband's quality of life is on the line. Your quality of life is on the line. Your children's quality of life is on the line. Don't give up! Keep Fighting!

War Weapon: Joshua 1:9

"Have I not commanded you? Be strong and courageous. Do not be frightened, and do not be dismayed, for the LORD your God is with you wherever you go."

My thoughts/feelings about today

_____

_____

_____

_____

_____

_____

_____

Day 9

His Release and Rescue

The word of God says in Luke 10: 17-19, *"The seventy-two returned with joy and said, 'LORD, even the demons submit to us in your name.' He replied, 'I saw Satan fall like lightning from heaven. I have given you authority to trample on snakes and scorpions and to overcome all the power of the enemy; nothing will harm you."*

So based on your Word and on the power of your name, I'm asking you to release your deliverance. Release your healing. Release your mercy. Release your grace. Release your favor. Release your power. Release your anointing. Release your protection. Bind every demonic assignment off of my husband's life. Be a shield. Be a comforter. Be a provider. Don't allow him to sit in the background. Help him have the courage to step into the forefront with confidence in his ability to lead his family effectively. Lord, I cry out to you on his behalf. I know you don't want to see him sinking in sin, making bad decisions and living outside of your will for his life. So be a present help during this time of distress, confusion, and pain. Rescue him. Rescue us. Don't delay God. In Jesus name, I pray. Amen.

Wisdom for Wives

Wise counsel is necessary during war. Proverb 24:6 says *"Surely you need guidance to wage war, and victory is won through many advisers."* That's why there is a hierarchy in militaries. You need someone with more experience than you to help you develop the appropriate strategy without wasting all of your time, resources, and energy trying to figure out how to fight effectively. So find 1-2 trusted people who can offer you encouragement and support during this difficult time.

War Weapon: Proverbs 19:20 (ESV)

"Listen to advice and accept instruction, that you may gain wisdom in the future."

My thoughts/feelings about today

_____

_____

_____

_____

_____

_____

_____

Day 10

Healing from His Past

Free my husband from the feelings of betrayal from those who were supposed to love, nurture, protect, and support him. May he recognize their failure was not due to any deficiency in him but due to reasons they themselves aren't able to articulate or acknowledge. Free him from the desire to have answers that will never be available or would be insufficient to justify the pain he suffered. Give him a heart and mind to forgive so the enemy doesn't find a way to keep him from moving forward or from fully enjoying his life.

I ask that you heal him so that old wounds never bleed again. Help him so he knows he can count on you to always be in his corner. Strengthen him in areas where he feels weakest. Contend with those forces that contend with him. Love him in ways he's never experienced love. Nurture him so he never feels empty. Be his defense in every battle so he never feels forsaken. Be his fortress and refuge for every storm so he always feels protected (Psalm 18:2). In Jesus name, I pray. Amen.

Wisdom for Wives

You can't fight while scrolling Facebook. You can't fight while posting pics on Instagram. You don't see soldiers on the battlefield with a cell phone so they can keep up with the latest celebrity gossip. War time is serious. War can be deadly so you had better show up wielding the right weapon. Put the phone down and get on your face before God. Get your priorities in order. Get your household affairs in order instead of trying to keep up with how everyone else is living.

War Weapon: 1 Peter 5:8

"Be sober-minded; be watchful. Your adversary the devil prowls around like a roaring lion, seeking someone to devour."

My thoughts/feelings about today

_____

_____

_____

_____

_____

_____

_____

Day 11

His Direction

Make my husband uncomfortable in his lack of direction, transparency, or integrity. Don't allow him to walk around aimlessly and without a spiritual, financial, mental, emotional, or physical plan for his and his family's well-being. May he see the gifts that you've placed on the inside of him and work diligently and consistently to develop those gifts so they are used the way you intended. Don't allow the enemy of low self-esteem, pride, addiction, or selfishness interfere with your plans for him.

He needs you in ways he can't even express. He needs you when things are going well and when the bottom falls out. He needs you to come down personally on his behalf. He needs a personal miracle. He needs a personal intervention from you. He isn't going to make it without you. He is sinking due to sin, distress, frustration, and all kinds of other things. Deliver him now. Intervene now. Show up NOW. Lord, don't delay! In Jesus name, I pray. Amen.

Wisdom for Wives

Don't leave your life partner to face war by himself. Yes, he is an adult. Yes, he should be able to fight for his own healing and deliverance. But the word of God says that *"it is not good that man should be alone. I will make him a suitable helper"* (Genesis 2:18). That is *you*. You are the suitable helper that God has sent to help your husband become the man that God created. He won't make it without you. He won't be healed without your prayers. He won't be delivered without your support. Be his suitable helper.

War Weapon: Proverbs 27:17

"As iron sharpens iron, so one person sharpens another."

My thoughts/feelings about today

_____

_____

_____

_____

_____

_____

_____

Day 12

Help from God

Lord, my husband needs your wisdom, protection, peace, and guidance. He needs you to shield him from the plans of the enemy and protect him; cover him; and be his strength and fortress. I cry out to you God! Be the Lord of his life. Be his Savior. Heal him where he is hurting. Strengthen him to choose righteousness over foolishness. Help him overcome temptation by calling on your name. Turn back any plans to chastise him and show him mercy.

Lord, in all of his decision making, may he be led back to you. Don't let him stray. Don't let the enemy prevail. Don't let him crumble, stumble, or fall away from your presence, power, or peace. He needs you even during the times when he thinks he can handle things on his own and during the times he doesn't call on you. Be a very present help during times of struggle and times of success. Don't forsake your covenant with him (Deuteronomy 31:8). In Jesus name, I pray. Amen.

Wisdom for Wives

Can you imagine the anxiety and distress that Moses and the Israelites felt as they approached the Red Sea with Pharaoh's army in hot pursuit? They were in the will of God, following God's instructions and trusting His plan. Yet, they had to face obstacles that seemed daunting and that seemed impossible to survive. When Moses called out to God, God gave him instructions on what to do.

God's instructions seemed like a solution that wasn't really a practical solution. And the same is true when God instructs you. Sometimes, what God proposes won't seem like the answer that you are looking for or that it will yield the results that you want. The Word says, "*If you are willing and obedient, you will eat the good of the land*" (Isaiah 1:19). So learn to obey God's instructions, even when they don't make sense or seem practical.

War Weapon: 1 Peter 1:14

"As obedient children, do not conform to the evil desires you had when you lived in ignorance."

My thoughts/feelings about today

_____

_____

_____

_____

_____

_____

_____

Day 13

His Transformation

Lord, I call heaven down on behalf of my husband. His mindset cannot remain the same. His actions and inaction cannot remain the same. His attitude can't remain the same. There is too much at stake for him to not play the part he was meant to play as the leader of this family. Our future is on the line. Our children's lives are on the line. I need my husband to lead this household. I need him to lead our children. I need him to be an example of a surrendered Christ-centered life, hard work, and consistent effort, to our kids. He has to rise up and take his place. Constantly talk to him, convict him when he is wrong, put him on the right path when he strays, help him when he struggles, strengthen him when he's tempted, and help him when he's discouraged, lost or confused. Be a very present help in all situations and circumstances (Psalm 46:1). Show him how to lead in love, truth, honesty, and integrity; and may he take his role seriously and not be led astray by others who want to see him fall. In Jesus name, I pray. Amen.

Wisdom for Wives

_____ is a man after God's own heart. He is a man of integrity and forthrightness. He is the head and not the tail (Deuteronomy 28:13). He is complete and a whole new creature in Christ (2 Corinthians 5:17). His desire is to please God and follow after righteousness. He is mature and able to lead his family and pursue his calling. He is healed. His past no longer rules over his thoughts or view of himself and others. He is everything that you created him to be. I declare this over his life.

This is the type of prayer that you should be praying over your husband. This is the type of faith confession that should proceed from your mouth when you speak about your husband and when you speak to your husband. Your words have power, use them wisely.

War Weapon: Matthew 6:6

"But when you pray, go into your room and shut the door and pray to Father who is in secret. And your Father who sees in secret will reward you."

My thoughts/feelings about today

_____

_____

_____

_____

_____

_____

_____

Day 14

His Sin

Lord, I'm praying for the stirring of my husband's spirit so that he has to make changes before he experiences peace. I'm praying that he will have a yearning to walk with you, to be in your presence, and get his instructions from you. I pray that he will be led by your Spirit. Don't let pride keep him from seeking your face or your will. May he desire to commune with you, fellowship with you, and have a surrendered heart before you. Don't allow him to have sweet sleep until he repents. Don't allow him to overlook the pain he is causing or to have peace until he seeks your forgiveness. Take away the illusion of joy and fun that his sins seem to provide. Don't allow his spirit to be quiet but allow it to forever compel him to turn from his wicked ways. May he cry out to you in a way that causes you to move quickly. I'm not seeking vengeance, I'm seeking a repentant heart and I know that you are the only one who is able to change the heart of any person. So this is my prayer. May his sin weigh him down to the point that he seeks you, begging for relief. And when he seeks you, grant him the desires of his heart. In Jesus name, I pray. Amen.

Wisdom for Wives

Seek God like you've never sought Him before. Pray a different prayer. Worship from the depths of your pain and despair. Cry out for wisdom.

Recite a different scripture. Sing a new song. Go higher. Go deeper. God is calling you to a different level of maturity. He wants to see you grow. He is preparing you to receive all of the things you have prayed for.

War Weapon: Colossians 4:2

"Continue steadfastly in prayer, being watchful in it with thanksgiving."

My thoughts/feelings about today

_____

_____

_____

_____

_____

_____

_____

Day 15

Standing Against the Forces of Evil

God, I'm praying for the release of the spirit that has kept my husband in bondage. Deliver like only you can. Set him free like only you can. Bind every demonic spirit and evil force that has been assigned to steal his joy, peace, identity, family, and ministry. Fight those battles on his behalf. Show yourself as mighty in battle. Give him a desire to seek you to be released from this prison that sin has kept him in.

I pray against evil forces, influences, and his circle of friends that keep him from totally surrendering to you. Surround him with people who are after your own heart. Give him wisdom for every friendship and don't allow him to be led astray by those that the enemy tries to position to interfere with the work you want him to do. Keep him when he doesn't want to be kept. Keep him from the hands and plans of the enemy. I bind all the enemy's attempts to take what you have given or to destroy what you are building. In Jesus name, I pray. Amen.

Wisdom for Wives

Why go for the kill when it comes to how you treat your husband? You've already proven you can defeat him verbally, spiritually, and emotionally. Instead of killing him, feed him. Feed him with kindness, respect, and admiration. If you take care of his spirit, you will never war again.

War Weapon: 1 Timothy 2:8

"I desire then that in every place the men should pray, lifting holy hands without anger or quarreling."

My thoughts/feelings about today

_____

_____

_____

_____

_____

_____

_____

_____

Day 16

His Struggle with Sin

Don't allow the plans of the evil one to prevail in my husband's life. Show yourself mighty in battle on his behalf and on behalf of our family.

I pray against any and all sin that my husband can't seem to break free from on his own. I know the wages of sin is death but I need him to live so he can fulfill his life's work. Don't allow sin to drown him. Don't allow sin to keep him hostage. Don't allow sin to cause him to make decisions that would take him off course from his purpose. May he be repulsed by sinful thoughts and behaviors. May he run from sin as if his life depended on it. May he feel burdened when he gives in to his sin until he lets it go and repents before you. In Jesus name, I pray. Amen.

Wisdom for Wives

Luke 6:28 says, *"Bless those who curse you, pray for those who mistreat you."*

I know it seems unfair. I know it feels like a burden. I know you are ready to give up, but find a way to keep pushing. Push past those feelings and negative thoughts. You have come so far. You have invested so much. Don't walk away before you get the breakthrough.

War Weapon: Matthew 7:7

"Ask, and it will be given to you; seek, and you will find; knock, and it will be opened to you."

My thoughts/feelings about today

_____

_____

_____

_____

_____

_____

_____

Day 17

His Rebellion

Lord, I need you to come in and clean this stuff up and clear this stuff out—all of this rebellion, selfishness, and ungodly habits and mindsets. I need your help. My husband and leader needs your help. Our children need your help. We are lost without you. We are powerless without you. We need you desperately.

I need him to act in the capacity for which he was assigned. I'm so tired of fighting alone; so tired of being the one to develop strategies, carry the load, and fight to save the family while he is rogue. Clear my husband's distorted ways of seeing things. Allow your truth to penetrate every area of his life. May he be a truth seeker and find the truth by studying your Word. Uproot all of the lies that the enemy has implanted to keep him from greatness and from becoming all that you envisioned

Bring him back stronger than ever with wisdom and understanding that he's never had before. With the fear of the Lord guiding his every decision, help him develop a ready, alert and made-up mind to do what pleases you. In Jesus name, I pray. Amen.

Wisdom for Wives

Please understand that the enemy comes to kill, steal and destroy but Jesus has come to give life more abundantly (John 10:10). Trust that you and your husband will see good days. Trust that God will restore the years that the locusts have eaten up (Joel 2:25). Trust that as you sow good things into your husband, good things will come back to you as his wife (Galatians 6:7-8). Fully trust God's word and His promises.

War Weapon: John 16:23b-24

"Truly, truly, I say to you, whatever you ask of the Father in my name, he will give it to you. Until now you have asked nothing in my name. Ask, and you will receive, that your joy may be full."

My thoughts/feelings about today

_____

_____

_____

_____

_____

_____

_____

Day 18

His Insecurity and Feelings of Inadequacy

I speak to every insecurity and all feelings of inadequacy and call on the Spirit of God to cover them, uproot them, and bind them so they never rise again. I release every demonic hold and spirit that threatens to keep my husband in bondage. I cover his heart, mind, soul and spirit with the precious blood of Jesus Christ because nothing trumps the blood and the blood never loses its power. I call out every demonic force that is waging war inside of my husband. I speak healing, deliverance, and peace over all of the broken, insecure, unsettled places in his heart. I call on God's Angels in heaven to join forces with my husband to fight the enemy that is seeking to destroy his life. May my husband realize that worship is his way out of any stronghold that he has within him. May he worship from the depths of his soul even during those times when he doesn't believe worship is enough to help him overcome life's challenges. May he learn to call on you morning, noon and night so the plans of the enemy don't prevail against him. Give him strength to fight even when he is weary. In Jesus name, I pray. Amen.

Wisdom for Wives

You don't want to see or think about your husband in a negative way. You don't want to have the wrong attitude towards him. Ask God to speak to the hurt, disappointment, and restlessness brewing inside of you. Don't grow weary in well doing. The word of God says you will reap if you don't faint (Galatians 6:9). God knows you get tired of having to be strong, understanding and leading the battles on your own. He understands that you need more from your life partner. God is your help. He is your Source. He is your Resource. Trust Him as He works behind the scenes to make things right.

War Weapon: Proverbs 3:5-6

"Trust in the Lord with all your heart and lean not on your own understanding; in all your ways submit to him, and he will make your paths straight."

My thoughts/feelings about today

_____

_____

_____

_____

_____

_____

_____

Day 19

His Fears

God, my husband can't afford to sit on the sidelines and let me do the heavy lifting. I need you to work through him to help change this situation around.

He may not feel like he is competent enough to do all that you've called him to do. He may feel overwhelmed by the responsibilities you've placed on his shoulders. He may be scared that he will fall short or make a wrong decision. May he surrender all of those feelings and fears to you. May he seek you for wisdom, direction, and discretion in all of his decision making (Proverbs 3:5). Show me how to extend grace to him during the times he doesn't make the best decisions and continue to offer encouragement and kind words, so he doesn't lose confidence in himself. May he find his adequacy by looking to and leaning on you. In Jesus name, I pray. Amen.

Wisdom for Wives

Right now, you probably won't feel like fighting. You'll be tempted to lay down and quit. You'll feel like the weight of the world is on your shoulder. That's part of every battle. Get up and fight another day, pray harder, seek support, worship more, and vent to trusted support system. But don't quit! This is not the time to walk away!

War Weapon: Romans 12:12

"Rejoice in hope, be patient in tribulation, be constant in prayer."

My thoughts/feelings about today

_____

_____

_____

_____

_____

_____

_____

Day 20

His Wholeness

Lord, rain down healing on my husband so he can be made whole. May he seek you with his whole heart so he can find the peace, comfort and answers he needs to face life's toughest challenges (Jeremiah 29:3). Send your Angels his way. May he not be too prideful to ask and seek out help. Show him how to trust the right people—people that walk with you and who fear your name. Surround him with godly men who can teach him, hold him accountable, offer wise counsel, support him, laugh with him, enjoy his company, and pour into him. May there be no voids or deficits in his life. Hear the cries of his soul when he hesitates to ask for what he needs and deliver him from all of his distresses. Save his life before his sin, fears, worries, and insecurities threaten to take it. I pray that he will allow you to heal him. His family needs his leadership and guidance. We need him to make sound decisions. We need him to have a plan for our present and our future. I want to be in a supportive role, not an adversarial role. Show us how to be team mates working towards the same goal, moving our family forward. We can't afford to waste any more time, energy, or resources. Changes are needed right now. God, you are the only one who can change the heart of people so I ask that you would change our hearts towards you and towards each other.

May we treat each other as an asset instead of a liability. May we support, encourage, help, and prioritize your will above our own. Unite our hearts and help us to be on one accord. In Jesus name, I pray. Amen.

Wisdom for Wives

Sometimes it's your negative thought life that keeps you dazed, discouraged, and confused. This journey will require you to actively challenge your pattern of negative thinking. The Bible says to take your thoughts captive (2 Corinthians 10:5) for a reason. Negative thoughts lead to negative emotions which feed your feelings of hopelessness. It's a cycle that needs to be interrupted as soon as you are aware that you've entered the cycle. That's why faith confessions and speaking God's word consistently is so powerful. They counteract negative thoughts.

War Weapon: Philippians 4:8

"Finally, brothers, whatever is true, whatever is honorable, whatever is just, whatever is pure, whatever is lovely, whatever is commendable, if there is any excellence, if there is anything worthy of praise, think about these things."

My thoughts/feelings about today

_____

_____

This is War

_____

_____

_____

_____

_____

Day 21

His Future

Open his eyes that he may have a clear vision for his future and for the future of this family. Sear it in his heart and mind so he doesn't lose focus on what he has been called to do as the leader of our home. Don't let him be led astray with foolishness, distractions, ungodly people, or anything that would hinder his ability/willingness to lead. May he not grow weary, get discouraged, or walk away from this assignment. May he study, seek wise counsel, pray, and continuously look to the hills from whence comes his help (Psalm 121:1-2). May he redeem the time, for the days are evil (Ephesians 5:16). In Jesus name, I pray. Amen.

Wisdom for Wives

Implement a new marriage strategy today. Do something positive that you wouldn't normally do. It could be deciding to refrain from complaining or nagging. It could be catering to the needs of your spouse today. It could be writing a note of gratitude to your spouse. You could compliment your spouse or apologize for any disrespectful behavior. This entire journey is geared towards helping you do things differently than you've done them in the past. So today be intentional about making a small step towards having a new marriage.

War Weapon: Colossians 3:12

"Therefore, as God's chosen people, holy and dearly loved, clothe yourselves with compassion, kindness, humility, gentleness and patience."

My thoughts/feelings about today

_____

_____

_____

_____

_____

_____

_____

Day 22

His Healing

Heal his eyes so he doesn't focus on anything or anyone that will hinder his destiny (Psalm 119:37).

Heal his heart so he can freely give and receive the outpouring of love that you and others want to offer (Ezekiel 36:26).

Heal his ears so he only listens to wise and godly counsel (Proverbs 11:14).

Heal his hands so that he works onto the Lord and not onto men that he may receive a good reward for his labor (Colossians 3:23).

Heal his mouth so that only words that edify and are kind proceed out (Ephesians 4:29).

Heal his mind so that he meditates on your Word and whatever is pure and of a good report (Philippians 4:8).

Heal his feet so that he doesn't walk unrighteously before you or get caught in some hidden trap laid by the enemy (Psalm 31:4).
In Jesus name, I pray. Amen.

Wisdom for Wives
Pray this prayer for yourself today:

Lord,

When I'm weary, strengthen me.

When I'm discouraged, be my motivation.

When I'm in despair, be my hope.

When I'm restless, be my peace.

I don't want to drown while trying to help my husband. I don't want to feel forgotten about why I stand strong for this marriage and exercise my faith.

I don't want to get depressed while waiting on deliverance. I need you just as badly he does. It's hard to stand and fight when my partner is not standing with me and sometimes against me.

So in all of your healing and help, please Lord don't forget about me.

In Jesus name, I pray. Amen.

War Weapon: 1 Chronicles 16:11

"Seek the LORD and his strength; seek his presence continually!"

My thoughts/feelings about today

_____

_____

_____

_____

_____

_____

_____

This is War

Day 23

His Wife's Declaration

Lord, your Word says, *"For our struggle is not against flesh and blood, but against the rulers, against the authorities, against the powers of this dark world and against the spiritual forces of evil in the heavenly realms"* (Ephesians 6:12).

So I confess today that my husband is not my enemy.

And I stand firmly against the enemy of infidelity.

I stand against the enemy of deceit.

I stand against the enemy of childhood wounds that continue to plague my husband and marriage.

I stand against the enemy of addiction.

I stand against the enemy of spiritual immaturity.

I stand against the enemy of financial irresponsibility.

I will not position myself against my husband. Instead, I stand against demonic forces at work in his life. I stand against any person, place, or thing that keeps him from living life the way God intended. I stand against any negative thoughts that color his view of himself, his marriage, and his abilities. I stand firmly beside him as his life partner even during the times he is not planted as firmly next to me.

I won't allow the enemy to use me to divide our home regardless of what my husband chooses to do.

My desire is to please God and to follow His instructions, so I won't miss the blessings and peace.

In Jesus name, I pray. Amen.

Wisdom for Wives

This is your calling at this time, in this season, for the greater good of your family. Draw your strength and encouragement from God who promises to sustain you during difficult times. You can't afford to crumble. You can't afford to sit in the middle of the battlefield while war is raging all around you. You can't afford to give up and walk away because the dissolution of this relationship has far-reaching impact.

War Weapon: 1 Peter 5:7

"Cast the whole of your care [all your anxieties, all your worries, all your concerns, once and for all] on Him, for He cares for you affectionately *and* cares about you watchfully."

My thoughts/feelings about today

_____

_____

_____

_____

_____

_____

Day 24

His Bondage

Lord, according to your Word, "*Opponents must be gently instructed, in the hope that God will grant them repentance leading them to a knowledge of the truth, and that they will come to their senses and escape from the trap of the devil, who has taken them captive to do his will*" (2 Timothy 2:25-26).

So in the name of Jesus, I pray that you would release the noose that is around my husband's neck which is trying to choke the life out of him spiritually, emotionally, mentally, and financially. Loose him from every chain that keeps him in bondage. This is a war our family cannot afford to lose. This is a war that your Kingdom cannot afford to lose. You've created my husband to impact your Kingdom and your people in a positive way. We need you to be his commander-in-chief. Be his confidant. Be his strength. And fight on his behalf! In Jesus name, I pray. Amen.

Wisdom for Wives

Did you really think the enemy would give up without a fight? Do you think he will lay down and allow you to get the victory? Don't be surprised at the resistance. It's normal to resist threats that don't align with our own agendas or goals. No one wants to be defeated. So you shouldn't expect anything less from your enemy. Everyone wants to win.

Just as you are using every weapon you can think of to win, so is your enemy. Just as you have developed a strategy, so has your enemy. This is a battle field, not a softball tournament! You have trained or are training for this. Remember, your enemy has had the advantage for much longer than you've even been around. He knows what will work, but what he is missing is the power of God. You have supernatural advantage that the enemy will not be able to defeat.

War Weapon: Ephesians 6:13-18

"Therefore, put on the full armor of God, so that when the day of evil comes, you may be able to stand your ground, and after you have done everything, to stand. Stand firm then, with the belt of truth buckled around your waist, with the breastplate of righteousness in place, and with your feet fitted with the readiness that comes from the gospel of peace. In addition to all this, take up the shield of faith, with which you can extinguish all the flaming arrows of the evil one. Take the helmet of salvation and the sword of the Spirit, which is the word of God. And pray in the Spirit on all occasions with all kinds of prayers and requests."

My thoughts/feelings about today

_____

_____

_____

This is War

_____

_____

_____

_____

Day 25

His Ultimate Need

God, I ask that you would save my husband from himself. He doesn't have enough of your power to stop this downward trajectory on his own. So I call down the power of God on his behalf. My husband can't keep ignoring challenges and hoping for the best. He can't keep his head in the sand and not address the issues that keep following and affecting him and his family. The enemy is going to destroy him if he doesn't armor up. Save him from his own folly and foolishness. Give me a life partner that is healthy, whole, healed, strong, delivered, surrendered, mature, loving, kind, consistent, faithful, trustworthy, honest, fun, wise, humble, and responsible; willing to seek you, lead his family towards your plan, and pour into his wife and children, thus portraying himself as someone worth following. I pray that he will humble himself, pray, seek your face, and turn from his wicked ways so you will forgive him and heal everything around him (2 Chronicles 7:14). In Jesus name, I pray. Amen.

Wisdom for Wives

War time is dangerous. War can cause many casualties if one is not careful. There were many times I felt like my efforts would never pay off and I got so tired of fighting. There always seemed to be a battle and it felt like I was the only one who discerned them when they showed up. I was having my own internal battle because I wasn't getting much in return for my efforts. I had to constantly ask God to free me from bondage and to release the chains from around my heart so I'd be authentic and consistent in my interactions with my husband. I wanted to do it God's way so I was always praying that God wouldn't allow me to get destroyed in this process of fighting on behalf of my life partner. That's why it's critically important that you get your instructions from God and from wise counsel. Don't try to fight without a proper battle strategy.

War Weapon: Proverbs 4:13

"Keep hold of instruction; do not let go; guard her, for she is your life."

My thoughts/feelings about today

_____

_____

_____

_____

_____

_____

_____

Day 26

His Desires and Thoughts

I declare that all generational curses are powerless and have no influence in my husband's life or decision making. I curse all generational curses at the root so they may never rise again. I need my husband to be awake, alert, and on guard at all times. I don't need him to give in to every temptation or negative thought he has. I need him to weigh the consequences and count the cost before he makes any decision. I need him to seek you in ways he never has. I need him to realize that he needs you at all times. I need him to fear you. I need him to pursue you. I need him to sit with you. I need him to be led by you. I don't want him to be satisfied with living on crumbs but whole bread, to live like an heir to the throne of grace, mercy and riches. In Jesus name, I pray. Amen.

Wisdom for Wives

Self-care is the word of the day. Soak in a bubble bath with soft music playing in the background. Go visit a friend. Get a manicure or a massage. Go to a movie. Do whatever nurtures you and feeds your soul. War time is draining. Be sure to take care of yourself during this difficult time.

War Weapon: Psalm 3:5

"I lie down and sleep; I wake again, because the LORD sustains me."

My thoughts/feelings about today

_____

_____

_____

_____

_____

_____

_____

Day 27

His Deliverance

We need an intervention from you right away God. Don't tarry, come now, deliver now, heal now, help now, grant favor now, give peace now, lead now, and save now. Hear my humble cries Lord. This is a war we cannot afford to lose. There's too much at stake and we need our most powerful warhead for this battle. You are that warhead. Strike down discouragement. Strike down fear. Bring down strongholds and generational curses. We set our eyes towards heaven because we need you in the worst way. Please, don't be slow to respond. We need more than a glimmer of hope. We need full-fledged deliverance and help. On this battlefield, the enemy is fighting us on every side; but you surround us on every side. The enemy is trying to make us Prisoners of War. We are soldiers in your army. Don't let go of our hands. Send blessings of peace and prosperity. Allow us to collect the spoils from our enemy (2 Chronicles 20:25) as you make our enemy our footstool (Psalm 110:1). Restore the years that the locusts have eaten up (Joel 2:25). Bless us seven times more than we had as you did Job once he stood strong during his battle. Allow us to enjoy good days, days worth living for, as we set our gaze towards you.

Without you, there is no hope for reconciliation so be the foundation on which we build, so that our house is able to stand firm and strong this time around. In Jesus name, I pray. Amen.

Wisdom for Wives

Pray this prayer for today:

Lord, protect me as I commit to fighting this battle. I know the enemy will not fight fair. I know he will use things from my past to keep me from completing this assignment. I know that he seeks to find anything he can use to destroy my life. So I need you to cover me. Shield me. Protect me from the hands and plans of the enemy at all times. Carefully and affectionately watch over everything that concerns my family and me. Post your Angels all around us at all times. Don't ever let there be a time when we don't have your covering or protection.

War Weapon: Isaiah 41:10

"Fear not, for I am with you; be not dismayed, for I am your God; I will

strengthen you, I will help you, I will uphold you with my righteous

right hand.:

My thoughts/feelings about today

_____

_____

_____

This is War

_____

_____

_____

_____

Day 28

His Strength

Don't allow my husband to crumble from the weight of the pressure he feels. Be a very present help in trouble (Psalm 46:1). Show up before he asks. May he feel your presence at all times so he doesn't get discouraged and doesn't faint before he gets the breakthrough he is so desperate for. Condition him to seek you, your Word, your face, and your Kingdom at all times so he has strength to stand strong during times of despair and adversity. Show him how much he needs you, not through trials, tribulations, or challenges but simply by being in constant communication with him as your son. Have mercy when he doesn't deserve it. Be patient when he doesn't obey. Be a deliverer when he is hopeless. Be a compass when he loses his way. In Jesus name, I pray. Amen.

Wisdom for Wives

Pray this prayer today:

Lord, I cry out to you for immediate help and deliverance. Your Word says we have not because we ask not or we ask with wrong intention (James 4:2-3). Test my heart and see that my intentions are pure before you. My intentions are to save my husband's life and ministry, to free him from what hinders his walk and relationship with you. Be a very present help in the time of trouble (Psalm 46:1). In Jesus name, I pray. Amen.

War Weapon: Psalm 50:15

"And call upon me in the day of trouble; I will deliver you, and you shall glorify me."

My thoughts/feelings about today

_____

_____

_____

_____

_____

_____

_____

Day 29

His Money

God, I pray that you would change my husband's mindset on money. Show him how to be a good steward over what you've blessed him with (Proverbs 10:4). May he not spend unwisely. May he not be selfish but make him a cheerful giver (2 Corinthians 9:7). May he realize the importance of ensuring he positions his family for financial success and stability. May he see money as a tool. May he see it as a finite resource that should be managed responsibly to save for the future, take care of the present, bless others, and enjoy activities that replenish the soul. In Jesus name, I pray. Amen.

Wisdom for Wives

Get out and get physical today. Take a brisk walk, go to the gym, or go for a jog. You need to get out all of those pent-up emotions right now. Burn off some steam; reduce your stress level. You have to get some type of physical activity.

War Weapon: Philippians 4:6
"Be anxious for nothing, but in everything, by prayer and petition, with thanksgiving, present your requests to God."

My thoughts/feelings about today

_____

_____

_____

_____

_____

_____

_____

Day 30

His Relationship with Christ

God please draw my husband nearer than before so he can experience you in ways he's never experienced you before. Be the same water-walking, raising-the-dead, healing-the-sick, making-the-blind-see Jesus in my husband's life. Don't allow him to remain the same. We can't afford to lose this soldier to addictions, dishonesty, sickness, lack of godly wisdom, lack of direction, or any form of temptation. Only you can change things around. So speak to him constantly so he cannot deny that it's your voice in his ear. Instruct him. Guide him. Help him formulate a plan. Don't let him play small. Don't allow him to remain comfortable in his sin. Don't allow him to remain stagnant. Motivate him and give him a sense of urgency. In Jesus name, I pray. Amen.

Wisdom for Wives

War will impact you in ways you never thought possible. It will alter your mindset. It will produce wounds. It will make you fatigue. It will cause you to question if fighting is worth it. These are normal reactions. You will be uncomfortable. You will be pushed beyond your limitations. War will take a heavy toll on you. So don't be surprised at how weary, discouraged or fatigued you become during this time. Just remind yourself that you're fighting for a new husband, new marriage, to keep your family together and for your happily ever after.

War Weapon: Matthew 11:28-30

"Come to me, all who labor and are heavy laden, and I will give you rest. Take my yoke upon you, and learn from me, for I am gentle and lowly in heart, and you will find rest for your souls. For my yoke is easy, and my burden is light."

My thoughts/feelings about today

_____

_____

_____

_____

_____

_____

_____

_____

Closing Remarks

Well sis, you made it!

If you feel worn out, that's normal.

If you feel like you have been in the toughest fight of your life, that's normal.

War time is exhausting physically, mentally, spiritually, and emotionally. This journey has required a lot from you. If you are anything like me, you almost walked away a few times and frequently questioned if this was what God was calling you to do. Let's face it. Would God really want you to be in so much pain and distress? Did God really expect you to be the sacrificial lamb?

And all of this probably seemed really unfair and at times totally unrealistic! But you made it! You fought the good fight. You've stood strong! You faced your enemy head on. You've learned new strategies. And you've become a woman that you totally don't recognize. Hopefully, you've allowed this process to change and challenge you. Hopefully you've allowed it to mature you. None of your efforts has been in vain! It was necessary. You aren't the sacrificial lamb; rather, you are the conduit through which your husband will get healed and whole. God hasn't forgotten about you. You are equally important to God as your husband. You will get your reward!

If you haven't seen the changes you were hoping for, begin at Day 1 and keep fighting! Remember, the enemy has had your husband in bondage for so many years that it may take more than 30 days of prayer to get him released.

Be proud of yourself.

You have done well.

You are the type of soldier that God needs in his army!

Blessings Sis!

Made in the USA
Columbia, SC
21 November 2020

25113505R00050